OLYMPICS 84

written by BILL TANCRED
designed and illustrated by CHRIS REED
photographs by GEORGE HERRINGSHAW

Ladybird Books Loughborough

Table of contents
The 21 sports in the 1984 Games

Previous Olympic Games venues & dates

I	1896	Athens	April 6-15
II	1900	Paris	May 20-October 28
III	1904	St Louis	July 1-November 23
*	1906	Athens	April 22-May 2
IV	1908	London	April 27-October 31
V	1912	Stockholm	May 5-July 22
VI	1916	Berlin	Not held owing to War
VII	1920	Antwerp	April 20-September 12
VIII	1924	Paris	May 4-July 27
IX	1928	Amsterdam	May 17-August 12
X	1932	Los Angeles	July 30-August 14
XI	1936	Berlin	August 1-16
XII	1940	Tokyo, then Helsinki	Not held owing to War
XIII	1944	London	Not held owing to War
XIV	1948	London	July 29-August 14
XV	1952	Helsinki	July 19-August 3
XVI	1956	Stockholm	June 10-17
		Melbourne	November 22-December 8
XVII	1960	Rome	August 25-September 11
XVIII	1964	Tokyo	October 10-24
XIX	1968	Mexico City	October 12-27
XX	1972	Munich	August 26-September 10
XXI	1976	Montreal	July 17-August 1
XXII	1980	Moscow	July 19-August 3

1906 Games held to mark the 10th Anniversary of the modern games but not numbered since they were not held in the first year of the 1904-1908 Olympiad.

The Modern Olympic Games -How it started

Olympic stadium in Athens.
The site of the first modern Olympic Games in 1896

The world's greatest sporting spectacle was the idea of a French nobleman named Baron Pierre de Coubertin. During his travels around the world, Pierre de Coubertin was particularly impressed with the high interest in sports that he found in America and England. He could see no difference between the young men of these two countries and the young men of his native France, who at that time showed very little interest in sport generally.

It was after his travels that the Frenchman realised more than ever the truth of the ancient Greek ideal that the body, as well as the mind, must be cared for and improved.

He convinced the authorities that an Olympic Games was an excellent means of teaching the youth of the world international understanding.

Pierre de Coubertin set a fine example of how much one determined man can accomplish. To honour him and his ideals, some inspiring words that he had adopted from the Bishop of Pennsylvania were used as the official motto of the first games. These were –

The important thing in the Olympic Games is not to win but to take part; just as the important thing in life is not the triumph but the struggle. The essential thing is not to have conquered but to have fought well.

The Olympic events in 1984

ARCHERY

Archery is probably the oldest sport in the world and is thought to have become an organised sport in the 3rd century AD.

In the Olympics, the competitions are based on two rounds of 2 x 36 (72) arrows at the various ranges.

The men's ranges are 90 m, 70 m, 50 m and 30 m long. Maximum possible points total is 2,880. The women's ranges are 70 m, 60 m, 50 m and 30 m long. Again, the maximum possible points total is 2,880.

Today's world governing body is the Federation Internationale de Tir à l'Arc (FITA) which was founded in 1931. The 1984 competition will be held at *El Dorado Park.*

	1980 winner	Country	Points	Olympic record
Men	T Poikolainen	(Finland)	2,455	D Pace (USA) 2,571 pts
Women	K Losaberidze	(USSR)	2,491	L Ryon (USA) 2,499 pts

	1984 winner	Country	Points
Men	_____	_____	_____
Women	_____	_____	_____

Discus thrower Peter Tancred (GB)

ATHLETICS

The Greeks gave us athletics (track and field) which are probably the main attraction of the modern Olympic Games.

They began some 3,000 years ago with foot racing, to which was added later the throwing and jumping events.

The athletics events will be contested in the *Los Angeles Memorial Coliseum.*

Track

The track is 400 metres per lap in all eight lanes. Therefore, there are 'staggered' starting points for the 200 m, 400 m, 400 m hurdles, 800 m and the relays.

The 1,500 m is 3¾ laps; the 3,000 m and the 3,000 m steeplechase are both 7½ laps; the 5,000 m is 12½ laps; and the 10,000 m is 25 laps.

The 100 m, 100 m hurdles and 110 m hurdles are run on the straight.

The marathon starts and finishes in the athletics stadium and the distance is 42,195 m (26 miles and 385 yards.)

Events are timed using electronic apparatus which is correct to 1/100th of a second. This is how the official time is recorded for events up to and including 400 m.

Events from 800 m to 10,000 m are recorded to 1/10th of a second. The marathon is recorded to the whole second.

In starting an event, the starter's commands are— 'On

Allan Wells (GB) winning the 1980 Olympic 100 m

your marks' (in the starter's native language) and, for races up to 400 m, 'set.' As soon as the competitors are still, the pistol is fired. All competitors are allowed one warning for a false start and are disqualified for a second false start.

When finishing an event the winner is the first athlete to reach the finishing tape with any part of his or her **torso**. (This does not include the head, arms or feet.)

During the race itself, competitors must stay in their allocated lane (if any). Jostling and obstructing other competitors is not allowed. The track judges will disqualify athletes guilty of these offences.

Hurdles and steeplechase

There are ten *flights* in the four hurdle events. They are 1.067 m (3 ft 6 in) high for the men's 110 m, 0.91 m (3 ft) high for the men's 400 m and 0.84 m (2 ft 9 in) for the women's 100 m. For the new women's 400 m event the hurdles are 0.76 m (2 ft 6 in) high. Hurdles knocked down unintentionally do not result in disqualification. This could however make the hurdler slower.

In the steeplechase event there are twenty eight hurdle barriers and seven water jumps.

◁ *1980 Olympic 1,500 m final.*
279 Steve Ovett (GB) 257 Steve Cram (GB) 254 Sebastian Coe (GB)

	1980 winner and time	Olympic record and time	1984 winner and time
100 m			
Men	A Wells (GB) 10.25	J Hines (USA) 9.95	
Women	L Kondratyeva (USSR) 11.06	A Richter (FRG) 11.01	
200 m			
Men	P Mennea (Italy) 20.19	T Smith (USA) 19.83	
Women	B Wöckel (GDR) 22.03	B Wöckel (GDR) 22.03	
400 m			
Men	V Markin (USSR) 44.60	L Evans (USA) 43.86	
Women	M Koch (GDR) 48.88	M Koch (GDR) 48.88	
800 m			
Men	S Ovett (GB) 1:45.40	A Juantorena (Cuba) 1:43.50	
Women	N Olizaryenko (USSR) 1:53.5	N Olizaryenko (USSR) 1:53.5	
1,500 m			
Men	S Coe (GB) 3:38.40	K Keino (Kenya) 3:34.91	
Women	T Kazankina (USSR) 3:56.56	T Kazankina (USSR) 3:56.56	
3,000 m			
Women	New event		
5,000 m			
Men	M Yifter (Ethiopia) 13:21.0	B Foster (GB) 13:20.34	
10,000 m			
Men	M Yifter (Ethiopia) 27:42.7	L Viren (Finland) 27:38.35	

1 *Carl Lewis (USA) 100 m world champion (Helsinki)*
2 *Eamonn Coghlan (IRL) 5,000 m world champion (Helsinki)*
3 *Marita Koch (GDR) 400 m European champion*
4 *Steve Ovett (GB) 800 m Olympic champion 1980*
5 *Mary Decker (USA) 1,500 m world champion (Helsinki)*
6 *Jarmila Kratochvilova (TCH) 400 m world champion (Helsinki)*
7 *Sebastian Coe (GB) 1,500 m Olympic champion 1980*

13

1 José Marín (Spain)
30 km walk World best performance*

2 Robert de Castella (Australia) World marathon champion

3
Colin Reitz
(GB) left and
Patriz Ilg (FRG)
World champion
steeplechaser

	1980 winner and time	Olympic record and time	1984 winner and time
Marathon			
Men	W Cierpinski (GDR) 2:11:03 0	*W Cierpinski (GDR) 2:09:55.0	
Women	New event		
20 km walk			
Men	M Damilano (Italy) 1:23:35.5	*M Damilano (Italy) 1:23:35.5	
50 km walk			
Men	H Gauder (GDR) 3:49:24.0	*H Gauder (GDR) 3:49:24.0	
3,000 m steeplechase			
Men	B Malinowski (Poland) 8:09.70	A Gärderud (Sweden) 8:08.02	
110 m hurdles			
Men	T Munkelt (GDR) 13.39	R Milburn (USA) 13.24	

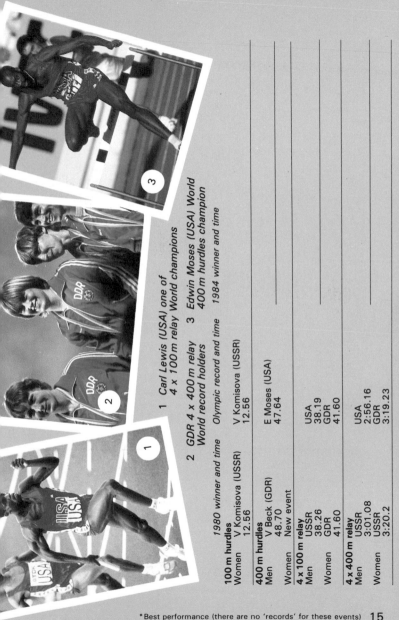

1 Carl Lewis (USA) one of 4 x 100 m relay World champions 3 Edwin Moses (USA) World 400 m hurdles champion

2 GDR 4 x 400 m relay World record holders

	1980 winner and time	Olympic record and time	1984 winner and time
100 m hurdles			
Women	V Komisova (USSR) 12.56	V Komisova (USSR) 12.56	
400 m hurdles			
Men	V Beck (GDR) 48.70	E Moses (USA) 47.64	
Women	New event		
4 x 100 m relay			
Men	USSR 38.26	USA 38.19	
Women	GDR 41.60	GDR 41.60	
4 x 400 m relay			
Men	USSR 3:01.08	USA 2:56.16	
Women	USSR 3:20.2	GDR 3:19.23	

Field events

A qualifying standard is set for all the field events. If athletes are successful at this stage, they proceed to the final. If less than twelve qualify, the number is made up to twelve. The finalists in the four throwing events and in the long and triple jumps have three trials. The first eight, after three trials, earn three additional trials.

Weights of implements for the throwing events are as follows:—

Shot	Discus	Javelin	Hammer
Men			
7.26 kg (16 lb)	2 kg (4 lb 6.55 oz)	800 g (28.22 oz)	7.26 kg (16 lb)
Women			
4 kg (8 lb 13 oz)	1 kg (2 lb 3.27 oz)	600 g (21.16 oz)	No women's event

Fatima Whitbread (GB)

In the long jump, the take-off board is 200 mm wide. A failure (red flag) arises if the jumper touches the ground or makes an impression on the Plasticine, beyond the far edge of the take-off board. The jump is measured from the take-off line to the nearest break in the sand made by any part of the body, including the limbs.

Carl Lewis (USA)

For the triple jump the rules are similar to the long jump except in the hopping phase. The athlete must land on the same foot as his take-off foot and in the 'step', land on the other foot. The trailing leg must not touch the ground. (Another name for this event is the hop, step and jump.)

In the high jump and pole vault events, two or more athletes often tie for first place, by clearing the same height. If a tie exists, the winner is the competitor with the fewest failures at that height.

If the tie still persists, the winner is the athlete with the fewest attempts at the lower heights. If a tie still exists between the competitors, it is only broken for first place, in which case competitors have one attempt at the height at which they were unsuccessful. If no decision results, then the bar is lowered and raised accordingly until the tie is broken and a winner is declared.

The field events

	1980 winner	Olympic record	1984 winner and result
High jump			
Men	G Wessig (GDR) 2.36 m	G Wessig (GDR) 2.36 m	
Women	S Simeoni (Italy) 1.97 m	S Simeoni (Italy) 1.97 m	
Long jump			
Men	L Dombrowski (GDR) 8.54 m	R Beamon (USA) 8.90 m	
Women	T Kolpakova (USSR) 7.06 m	T Kolpakova (USSR) 7.06 m	
Pole vault			
Men	K Kozakiewicz (Poland) 5.78 m	W Kozakiewicz (Poland) 5.78 m	
Triple jump			
Men	J Uudmäe (USSR) 17.35 m	V Saneyev (USSR) 17.39 m	
Shot			
Men	V Kiselyov (USSR) 21.35 m	V Kiselyov (USSR) 21.35 m	
Women	I Slupianek (GDR) 22.41 m	I Slupianek (GDR) 22.41 m	
Discus			
Men	V Rashchupkin (USSR) 66.64 m	M Wilkins (USA) 68.28 m	
Women	E Jahl-Schlaak (GDR) 69.96 m	E Jahl-Schlaak (GDR) 69.96 m	
Javelin			
Men	D Kula (USSR) 91.20 m	M Nemeth (Hungary) 94.58 m	
Women	M Colón (Cuba) 68.40 m	M Colón (Cuba) 68.40 m	

1 *Ramona Neubert (GDR) World heptathlon champion*

2 *Daley Thompson (GB) World decathlon champion*

3 *Ulrike Meyfarth (FRG) European high jump champion*

	1980 winner	*Olympic record*	*1984 winner and result*
Hammer			
Men	Y Svedikh (USSR) 81.80 m	Y Svedikh (USSR) 81.80 m	
Decathlon			
Men	D Thompson (GB) 8,495 pts	B Jenner (USA) 8,617 pts	
Heptathlon			
Women	New event		

BASKETBALL

The basketball competition is organised on a round by round basis for women and a group basis for men. Every nation plays every other in that group and the two teams with the largest number of points go forward to the semi-finals. At this stage the tournament is organised on a knock-out basis.

The venue for the competition will be **The Forum.**

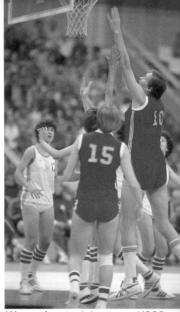

Women's match between USSR an Bulgaria at 1980 Olympics

	1980 winner	1984 winner
Men	Yugoslavia	_____
Women	USSR	_____

BOXING

The boxing competition involves eleven weight divisions organised on a knock-out basis. Each contest is boxed over three 3-minute rounds. The result depends on either a knock-out, the referee stopping the contest for the safety of the loser, or on a points decision.

The venue for these championships will be the **Los Angeles Sports Arena.**

Pat Cowdell (GB), boxing on the left, was a 1976 bronze medallist

The Divisions	1980 winner	1984 winner
Light flyweight (48 kg)	S Sabirov (USSR)	
Flyweight (Under 51 kg)	P Lessov (Bulgaria)	
Bantamweight (Under 54 kg)	J Hernández (Cuba)	
Featherweight (Under 57 kg)	R Fink (GDR)	
Lightweight (Under 60 kg)	A Herrera (Cuba)	
Light welterweight (Under 63.5 kg)	P Oliva (Italy)	
Welterweight (Under 67 kg)	A Aldama (Cuba)	
Light middleweight (Under 71 kg)	A Martinez (Cuba)	
Middleweight (Under 75 kg)	J Gómez (Cuba)	
Light heavyweight (Under 81 kg)	S Kačar (Yugoslavia)	
Heavyweight (81 kg +)	T Stevenson (Cuba)	

CANOEING

In the Olympics there are two types of canoeing: Kayaks and Canadian. In Kayak canoeing the canoeist uses a paddle with a blade at each end. The canoeist must use the left-hand blade on the left side and the right-hand blade on the right side of the kayak alternately, making a twisting and rolling movement with the body.

The Canadian paddle has only one blade, used on each side of the canoe alternately. Occasionally this type of canoeing is performed in a half-kneeling position for better propulsion.

The canoeing events will take place on *Lake Casitas.*

Lake Casitas

1 *Kayak singles*
2 *Canadian pairs*

Men	1980 winner	1984 winner
500 m Kayak singles	V Parfenovich (USSR)	
500 m Kayak pairs	USSR	
500 m Canadian singles	S Postrekhin (USSR)	
500 m Canadian pairs	Hungary	
1,000 m Kayak singles	R Helm (GDR)	
1,000 m Kayak pairs	USSR	
1,000 m Kayak fours	GDR	
1,000 m Canadian singles	L Lubenov (BUL)	
1,000 m Canadian pairs	Romania	
Women		
500 m Kayak singles	B Fischer (GDR)	
500 m Kayak pairs	GDR	

CYCLING

The cycling events are classified as track and road. In track events, the 1,000 metre time trial is against the clock. Competitors start off individually at intervals and the winner is the cyclist who completes the course fastest.

The Olympic Velodrome

The individual sprint consists of three laps contested by two or three cyclists. The winner is the cyclist with the fastest time over the last 200 m only, the earlier laps being for position.

In the 4,000 metre individual pursuit, two cyclists at a time compete for the honours. They start on opposite sides of the track. If a cyclist does not catch his opponent, the cyclist with the fastest time wins. The event itself is conducted on a knock-out system.

The 4,000 metre team pursuit involves teams of four cyclists who compete as in the individual pursuit. The winners are decided on the times of the first three cyclists of each team. One cyclist acts as a pacemaker.

In the road events, the individual road race is held over a predetermined course and does not involve the track.

The cycling events will be held at the **Olympic Velodrome.**

	1980 winner	Olympic record	1984 winner
1,000 m sprint	L Hesslich (GDR)	No record	
1,000 m time trial	L Thoms (GDR)	L Thoms (GDR) 1:02.95	
4,000 m individual pursuit	R Dill-Bundi (Switzerland)	R Dill-Bundi (Switzerland) 4:35.66	
4,000 m team pursuit	USSR	USSR 4:15.70	
Individual road race	S Sukhoruchenkov (USSR)	No record	
Team time trial	USSR	No record	
Women's individual road race	New event		

EQUESTRIAN

Equestrian sports include Grand Prix jumping, dressage and the three day event. Honours go to both individuals and teams.

Grand Prix (Show jumping)

In the individual Grand Prix jumping competition, competitors jump two rounds with the aggregate faults determining the winner. The first rounds normally have between twelve and fifteen obstacles not higher than 1.60 m (5 ft 3 in) or wider than 2.20 m (7 ft 2½ in), not including the water jump. The second round involves ten obstacles but the height may be increased.

In the team event, the course is identical to the first round of the individual event. The second round is contested by the best eight teams (only three out of four horses counting) over a course of six larger obstacles. The aggregate scores of the three best riders in each team over the two rounds decides the winner.

Dressage

The dressage discipline is organised to judge the understanding between the rider and the horse. The competition involves a variety of paces, halts, direction changes, movements and figures. Points are given for each skill, out of a maximum of ten. All competitors in the team competition must participate in the tests. The three team members with the highest aggregate scores are declared the winners. The best twelve riders then participate in the individual competition.

Three day event

This discipline includes the dressage, endurance test and show jumping. The individual and team (best three out of four in each team counts) competitions take place at the same time.

Show jumping at Montreal in 1976

	1980 winner	*1984 winner*
Three day event individual	F Roman (Italy)	
Three day event team	USSR	
Dressage individual	E Theurer (Austria)	
Dressage team	USSR	
Grand Prix jumping individual	J Kowalczyk (Poland)	
Grand Prix jumping team	USSR	

The above events will be held at *Santa Anita Park.*

27

FENCING

Historians estimate that swords have been used for about 5,000 years and fencing is one of the very few sports that cannot be proved to be directly related to the ancient Olympic movement.

The fencing competition involves both team and individual events with three weapons for men: foil, épée and sabre. There is only one weapon for women: the foil.

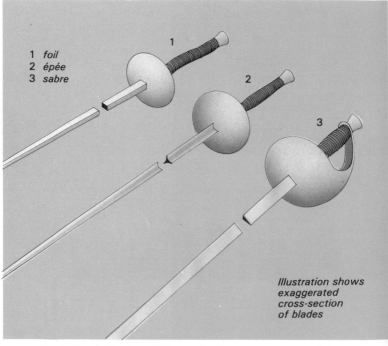

1 *foil*
2 *épée*
3 *sabre*

Illustration shows exaggerated cross-section of blades

Each discipline has different body target areas and the victor is the fencer scoring five hits (men) or four hits (women) in that specified region. The time limit is six minutes for men and five minutes for women.

The competition for the individual honours is organised on a pool system, while the team competition commences with a pool round but then becomes a knock-out competition.

The Olympic venue will be the **Long Beach Convention Centre.**

Wires attached to each competitor electronically record hits to the target area

Men	*1980 winner*	*1984 winner*
Individual foil	V Smirnov (USSR)	_____
Foil team	France	_____
Individual sabre	V Krovopouskov (USSR)	_____
Sabre team	USSR	_____
Individual épée	J Harmenberg (Sweden)	_____
Épée team	France	_____
Women		
Individual foil	P Trinquet (France)	_____
Foil team	France	_____

29

FOOTBALL (Association)

There are only sixteen teams who contest the medals at these Olympic games. To compete at these games, various qualifying matches are held at different venues throughout the world. The teams play on a group basis and get two points for a win, one for a draw, and zero for a loss. Players in the games *must* be amateurs although many Olympic footballers have gone on to become well-known professionals.

1980 winner

Czechoslovakia

1984 winner

Poland v Cuba in the 1976 Olympics

GYMNASTICS

There are eight events in the men's gymnastic competition. These include the floor exercises, pommel horse, rings, horse vault, parallel bars, horizontal bar, together with a team competition and the individual combined exercises. All competitors are marked out of a total of ten.

In the women's competition there are six events. These include the horse vault, asymmetric bars, balance beam, floor exercises, together with the team competition and the individual combined exercises. As in the men's competition, the women's events are marked out of a total of ten.

(It was interesting to see that at the last Olympics a maximum of ten was given to some gymnasts who demonstrated perfect skills.)

A new event has been included in this year's programme. This will be the rhythmic gymnastics competition shown below.

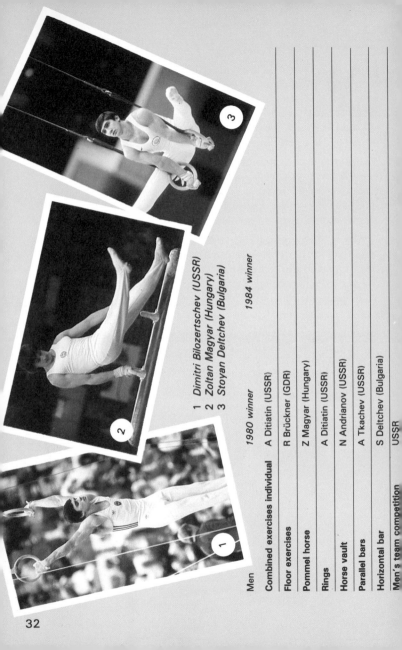

1 *Dimitri Bilozertschev (USSR)*
2 *Zoltan Magyar (Hungary)*
3 *Stoyan Deltchev (Bulgaria)*

Men	*1980 winner*	*1984 winner*
Combined exercises individual	A Ditiatin (USSR)	
Floor exercises	R Brückner (GDR)	
Pommel horse	Z Magyar (Hungary)	
Rings	A Ditiatin (USSR)	
Horse vault	N Andrianov (USSR)	
Parallel bars	A Tkachev (USSR)	
Horizontal bar	S Deltchev (Bulgaria)	
Men's team competition	USSR	

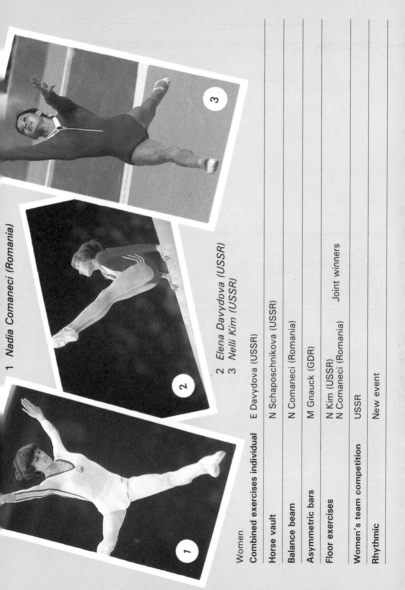

1 *Nadia Comaneci (Romania)*

Women			
Combined exercises individual	E Davydova (USSR)	2 Elena Davydova (USSR)	
		3 Nelli Kim (USSR)	
Horse vault	N Schaposchnikova (USSR)		
Balance beam	N Comaneci (Romania)		
Asymmetric bars	M Gnauck (GDR)		
Floor exercises	N Kim (USSR)	Joint winners	
	N Comaneci (Romania)		
Women's team competition	USSR		
Rhythmic	New event		

HANDBALL

This sport is a team game for twelve members of whom no less than five and no more than seven may be playing on court against the opposition.

The men's competition involves two 30-minute halves and women play two 20-minute halves with an interval of ten minutes for both men and women.

	1980 winner	*1984 winner*
Men	GDR	_____
Women	USSR	_____

Women's handball

HOCKEY (Field)

The game of hockey is played with two teams each having eleven players and two substitutes in case of injury or loss of form.

The actual tournament is organised with two pool systems, from which the two best teams in each pool progress to the next round. The event then becomes a knock-out competition.

To score a goal, the ball must pass into the opponent's net. The winning team receives two points. For a draw, both teams receive one point and no points are awarded to a losing team. Altogether the game is played over two 35-minute periods, with a ten-minute interval.

However, if a draw still exists after the final whistle in the semi-final and final stages of the competition, extra time is played. This involves two halves of seven and a half minutes each. If a draw still exists, then the team to score first is declared the winner.

	1980 winner	*1984 winner*
Men	India	_____
Women	Zimbabwe	_____

Spain v India in the 1980 final

35

Left: Neil Adams (GB) v Lehmann (GDR) in the 1980 semi-finals

JUDO

The sport of judo began as a means of self-defence. It is imperative to be strong with good balance and contests are normally won by the judoka showing greater holding and throwing techniques. The competition is held on a mat and the tournament is organised on an elimination basis. The contest in preliminary rounds lasts six minutes, semi-finals last eight minutes and the final lasts ten minutes.

The venue will be the *California State University, Los Angeles.*

Men	1980 winner	1984 winner
Up to 60 kg	T Rey (France)	
Up to 65 kg	N Solodukhin (USSR)	
Up to 71 kg	E Gamba (Italy)	
Up to 78 kg	S Khabareli (USSR)	
Up to 86 kg	J Röthlisberger (Switzerland)	
Up to 95 kg	R Van De Walle (Belgium)	
Over 95 kg	A Parisi (France)	
Open category	D Lorenz (GDR)	

The 1976 gold medallists in the team event.
Left to right: Jim Fox, Adrian Parker, Danny Nightingale (GB)

MODERN PENTATHLON

When the seventeenth Olympic games in ancient Greece finished, complaints that the Olympics did not have an all-round athletic competition for warriors were lodged by the war-like Spartans. Hence the pentathlon, a contest consisting of five events, was started in the eighteenth Olympics (708 BC). The competition included discus, long jump, javelin, running and wrestling.

Today, the five events in their competition order are: riding (800 m course), fencing (épée), shooting (pistol at 25 m), swimming (300 m freestyle), and cross country running (4,000 m).

Men	1980 winner	1984 winner
Individual	A Starostin (USSR)	
Team	USSR	

ROWING

The Chinese were the first to engage in the sport of long boat racing on rivers and tidal waters. To this day Chinese festivals include races between dragon boats or shallow draft boats, 22 m (73 ft) long, moved by twenty seven oarsmen.

To standardise the events and equipment, many obstacles had to be overcome. This sport has probably made more progress in equipment than any other sport and it is extremely difficult to keep the competition athletic rather than technological.

Coxless fours in the 1980 Olympics. USSR in red and GB who took the bronze medal

No Olympic records exist as water conditions vary from one Games to another.

The Olympic rowing events include:

Men	*1980 winner*	*1984 winner*
Single sculls	P Karppinen (Finland)	
Double sculls	GDR	
Coxless pairs	GDR	
Coxed pairs	GDR	
Four sculls with cox	GDR	
Coxless fours	GDR	
Coxed fours	GDR	
Eights	GDR	
Women		
Single sculls	S Toma (Romania)	
Double sculls	USSR	
Coxless pairs	GDR	
Four sculls with cox	GDR	
Coxed fours	GDR	
Eights	GDR	

East Germany's gold medallists in the 1980 coxed pairs

SHOOTING

The shooting competition involves the following disciplines: Olympic trap, running game, rapid fire pistol, skeet, free pistol, smallbore rifle (prone position) and smallbore (three positions).

In the free pistol competition, competitors fire sixty shots, in six series, from 50 m (164 ft). The target is similar to that for archery with the same scoring values but it is not coloured.

In the smallbore rifle (prone position) competition, competitors fire sixty shots from 50 m (164 ft) within two hours.

The smallbore rifle (three positions) involves the same equipment as above and the same target. The competitors however fire forty shots in four groups of ten shots, in each of three positions: standing, kneeling and prone.

Rapid fire pistol involves sixty shots at five targets from a distance of 25 m (82 ft). These shots are fired in groups of five, each at different targets which turn simultaneously from a side-on to face-on position and which are shown for a fifth of a second.

Running game target involves the competitors firing from 50 m (164 ft) through a 10 m (32 ft 9 in) wide opening at a normal run. Targets are shown for periods of five seconds. Competitors repeat this at a fast run when targets are shown for two and a half seconds. The target itself is shaped like a running boar and is divided into ten rings. The shots are fired in three groups of ten.

Trap shooting competitors use shotguns and fire at saucer-shaped clay targets. These targets are so designed that the flight is similar to that of a game bird at take-off. These 'game birds' are released in different directions from traps 15 m (49 ft 2½ in) away on the competitor's signal. Each competitor fires at 200 'game birds'. A hit is counted

Trap shooting – the simple trap shown in the inset gives an idea of how the 'game bird' is fired into the air

when the 'game bird' is visibly broken or reduced to dust. The competitor shoots from five shooting stations, in a line, 3.20 m (10 ft 6 in) apart.

Skeet shooting involves the same clay targets and shotgun. The shooting stations are in a semi-circular position and the 'game birds' are released from either one or both houses, together or separately. The competitors fire 200 shots and score as above.

Men	*1980 winner*	*1984 winner*
Olympic trap	L Giovanetti (Italy)	
Running game	I Sokolov (USSR)	
Rapid fire pistol	C Ion (Romania)	
Skeet	H Rasmussen (Denmark)	
Free pistol	A Melentyev (USSR)	
Smallbore (prone position)	K Varga (Hungary)	
Smallbore (three positions)	V Vlasov (USSR)	
Women		
Sport pistol	New event	
Air rifle	New event	
Smallbore (three positions)	New event	

SWIMMING

The Olympic pool is 50 m (54.68 yds) long and divided into eight lanes.

The Olympic competition will be held at the *Swim Stadium.*

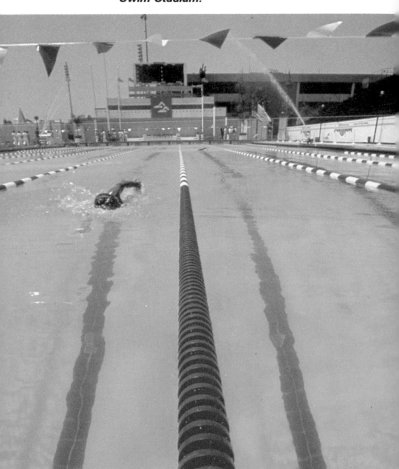

Swim Stadium

The swimmers compete in four events: freestyle (normally the crawl), backstroke, breaststroke and butterfly. The medley race, both individual and team, consists of the four named strokes over four equal distances.

Swimming events are organised on the basis of heats, semi-finals (if necessary) and a final. The swimmer with the fastest time in the heats or semi-final swims in the final, in lane 4 (centre), the next quickest, lane 5, the next lane 3 and so on. When seen on television, this explains the formation of an arrowhead. Three false starts constitute a disqualification.

Synchronised swimming has been added to this year's programme.

	1980 winner and time	Olympic record and time	1984 winner and time
100 m freestyle			
Men	J Woithe (GDR) 50.40	J Montgomery (USA) 49.99	
Women	B Krause (GDR) 54.79	B Krause (GDR) 54.79	
200 m freestyle			
Men	S Kopliakov (USSR) 1:49.81	S Kopliakov (USSR) 1:49.81	
Women	B Krause (GDR) 1:58.33	B Krause (GDR) 1:58.33	
400 m freestyle			
Men	V Salnikov (USSR) 3:51.31	V Salnikov (USSR) 3:51.31	
Women	I Diers (GDR) 4:08.76	I Diers (GDR) 4:08.76	
800 m freestyle			
Women	M Ford (Australia) 8:28.90	M Ford (Australia) 8:28.90	

	1980 winner and time	Olympic record and time	1984 winner and time
1,500 m freestyle			
Men	V Salnikov (USSR) 14:58.27	V Salnikov (USSR) 14:58.27	
100 m backstroke			
Men	B Baron (Sweden) 56.53	J Naber (USA) 55.49	
Women	R Reinisch (GDR) 1:00.86	R Reinisch (GDR) 1:00.86	
200 m backstroke			
Men	S Wladar (Hungary) 2:01.93	J Naber (USA) 1:59.19	
Women	R Reinisch (GDR) 2:11.77	R Reinisch (GDR) 2:11.77	
100 m breaststroke			
Men	D Goodhew (GB) 1:03.34	J Hencken (USA) 1:03.11	
Women	U Geweniger (GDR) 1:10.22	U Geweniger (GDR) 1:10.22	

David Wilkie (GB) during a 200 m breaststroke heat at the 1976 Games

200 m breaststroke

Men	R Shulpa (USSR) 2:15.85	D Wilkie (GB) 2:15.11
Women	L Kachushite (USSR) 2:29.54	L Kachushite (USSR) 2:29.54

100 m butterfly

Men	P Arvidsson (Sweden) 54.92	M Spitz (USA) 54.27
Women	C Metschuck (GDR) 1:00.42	K Ender (GDR) 1:00.13

200 m butterfly

Men	S Fesenko (USSR) 1:59.76	M Bruner (USA) 1:59.23
Women	I Geissler (GDR) 2:10.44	I Geissler (GDR) 2:10.44

400 m individual medley

Men	A Sidorenko (USSR) 4:22.89	A Sidorenko (USSR) 4:22.89
Women	P Schneider (GDR) 4:36.29	P Schneider (GDR) 4:36.29

4 x 100 m freestyle relay

Women	GDR 3:42.71	GDR 3:42.71
Men's event not held		USA 3:26.42

4 x 200 m freestyle relay

Men	USSR 7:23.50	USA 7:23.22

4 x 100 m medley relay

Men	Australia 3:45.70	USA 3:42.22
Women	GDR 4:06.67	GDR 4:06.67

Synchronised swimming duet figures

	New event

DIVING

The diving competitions consist of springboard and highboard events.

The dives on the international table have tariff values according to their degrees of difficulty. These range from 1.1 to 3.4. Marks in diving are out of ten.

For the Olympic competition there are seven judges and each dive is marked completely on merit without considering its degree of difficulty. The highest and lowest marks are discounted and the remainder are added together and multiplied by the degree of difficulty. This total is then given for the dive.

The diver must enter the water with his or her body straight, either feet or head first. Toes must be pointed with the feet together.

In the springboard competition, divers are required to make five compulsory dives and six voluntary (five for women). The voluntary dives must be chosen from five groups.

In the highboard competition, heats and a final are organised. Divers must execute four voluntary dives with the total of their degree of difficulty not exceeding 7.6 and six voluntary dives without limit (four for women).

Chris Snode (GB) 1980

The various diving boards and the judges sitting on high chairs

Men	*1980 winner*	*1984 winner*
Springboard	A Portnov (USSR)	
Highboard	F Hoffmann (GDR)	
Women		
Springboard	I Kalinina (USSR)	
Highboard	M Jäschke (GDR)	

WATER POLO

Water polo is a demanding team game played by two teams of up to eleven per side, of whom only seven from each team may be in the water at the same time. The game takes place in a pool measuring a minimum of 20 m x 8 m x 1.80 m deep (65 ft 7½ in x 26 ft 3 in x 5 ft 11 in).

The game itself lasts for four periods of five minutes with intervals of two minutes between each period. Competitors must play one-handed and punching is not allowed. The competition is organised on a group basis with three groups in the first round. The Olympic competition will be held at *Pepperdine University*.

	1980 winner	*1984 winner*
Men	USSR	

VOLLEYBALL

This game involves six players in each team and is played on a court with a high net. The main aim is to return the ball before it touches the ground. Points are obtained when the opposing team either hits the ball out of court or fails to return it before it touches the ground. Points are only given to the serving team and if the serving team is penalised, change of service is made to the opposing team who are then in a position to obtain points. Each match consists of the best of five sets. The team who gets fifteen points with a two point lead wins the set. Each team may touch the ball up to three times before it must go over the net to the opposing team.

The Olympic venue is the **Long Beach Sports Arena.**

	1980 winner	*1984 winner*
Men	USSR	_____
Women	USSR	_____

1980 Olympics. Brazil v Yugoslavia

49

WEIGHT LIFTING

The weight lifting gold medals can be won in ten different weight divisions. Each competitor attempts to lift the greatest weight correctly in two types of lifts: the snatch and the clean and jerk.

Vasili Alexeyev (USSR) lifting in the clean and jerk

The winner is the competitor who successfully lifts the greatest total weight employing these two methods. The weight lifter has up to three attempts at each weight and must succeed before attempting a greater weight. If two lifters tie having lifted the same total weight, the lightest one in body weight will be declared the Olympic champion.

Three judges decide on the rules and regulations regarding equipment and lifts executed. The Olympic venue is the *Loyola Marymount University*.

Weight class	1980 winner	Olympic record (Total weight)	1984 winner
Up to 52 kg	K Osmanoliev (USSR)	K Osmanoliev (USSR) 245 kg	
Up to 56 kg	D Nuñez (Cuba)	D Nuñez (Cuba) 275 kg	
Up to 60 kg	V Mazin (USSR)	V Mazin (USSR) 290 kg	
Up to 67.5 kg	Y Rusev (Bulgaria)	Y Rusev (Bulgaria) 342.5 kg	
Up to 75 kg	A Zlatev (Bulgaria)	A Zlatev (Bulgaria) 360 kg	
Up to 82.5 kg	Y Vardanyan (USSR)	Y Vardanyan (USSR) 400 kg	
Up to 90 kg	P Baczako (Hungary)	D Rigert (USSR) 382.5 kg	
Up to 100 kg	O Zaremba (TCH)	O Zaremba (TCH) 395 kg	
Up to 110 kg	L Taranenko (USSR)	L Taranenko (USSR) 422.5 kg	
Over 110 kg	S Rakhmanov (USSR)	V Alexyev (USSR) and S Rakhmanov (USSR) 440 kg	

WRESTLING

Two forms of wrestling exist for Olympic honours: free-style and Greco-Roman. Each consist of ten body weight classes. The Greco-Roman discipline restricts the use of legs. The actual competition is conducted on a 12 m (39 ft 4¼ in) square mat. Each bout is contested over three 3-minute rounds, unless a victory is obtained before that.

The competition will be held at the *Anaheim Convention Centre.*

Weight class Greco-Roman	1980 winner	1984 winner
Up to 48 kg	Z Ushkempirov (USSR)	
Up to 52 kg	V Blagidze (USSR)	
Up to 57 kg	S Serikov (USSR)	
Up to 62 kg	S Migiakis (Greece)	
Up to 68 kg	S Rusu (Romania)	
Up to 74 kg	F Kocsis (Hungary)	
Up to 82 kg	G Korban (USSR)	
Up to 90 kg	N Nottny (Hungary)	
Up to 100 kg	G Raikov (Bulgaria)	
Over 100 kg	A Kolchinsky (USSR)	

The Anaheim Convention Centre

Free-style wrestling

Free-style

Up to 48 kg	C Pollio (Italy)
Up to 52 kg	A Beloglazov (USSR)
Up to 57 kg	S Beloglazov (USSR)
Up to 62 kg	M Abuschev (USSR)
Up to 68 kg	S Absaidov (USSR)
Up to 74 kg	V Raitchev (Bulgaria)
Up to 82 kg	I Abilov (Bulgaria)
Up to 90 kg	S Oganesyan (USSR)
Up to 100 kg	I Mate (USSR)
Over 100 kg	S Andiev (USSR)

YACHTING

This sport consists of six different international classes. In each class there are seven races over a set course, usually marked by buoys. The fastest time wins. Yachts count their best six results from seven races and the winner is the yacht with the least number of points.

The classes	1980 winner	1984 winner
Soling (keelboat)	Denmark	_____
Star (keelboat)	USSR	_____
Flying Dutchman (centreboard dinghy)	Spain	_____
Finn (centreboard dinghy)	Finland	_____
470 (centreboard dinghy)	Brazil	_____
Tornado (catamaran)	Brazil	_____

Tornado class

This year, Board Sailing will be included in the yachting events. These will take place at the *Olympic Yachting Centre, Long Beach.*

1984 winner

Board Sailing   New event

Board Sailing

Representation at previous Olympic Games

Place	Year	Sports	Competitors	Nations
Athens	1896	10	311	13
Paris	1900	13	1330	22
St Louis	1904	12	625	13
London	1908	20	2056	22
Stockholm	1912	16	2546	28
Antwerp	1920	19	2692	29
Paris	1924	19	3092	44
Amsterdam	1928	16	3014	46
Los Angeles	1932	16	1408	37
Berlin	1936	21	4066	49
London	1948	18	4099	59
Helsinki	1952	17	4925	69
Melbourne	1956	18	3184	67
Rome	1960	18	5346	83
Tokyo	1964	20	5140	93
Mexico City	1968	18	5530	112
Munich	1972	21	7156	122
Montreal	1976	21	6085	92
Moscow	1980	21	5326	81

Los Angeles Coliseum, site of the 1984 Olympics. The opening and closing ceremonies and athletics events will take place here

57

World records

Athletics – Track and Field*

Men	Record	Holder	When achieved
100 m	9.93	Calvin Smith (USA)	1983
200 m	19.72	Pietro Mennea (ITA)	1979
400 m	43.86	Lee Evans (USA)	1968
800 m	1:41.73	Sebastian Coe (GB)	1981
1,500 m	3:30.77	Steve Ovett (GB)	1983
5,000 m	13:00.41	David Moorcroft (GB)	1982
10,000 m	27:22.4	Henry Rono (Kenya)	1978
Marathon	2:08.13	Alberto Salazar (USA)	1981
3,000 m st'chase	8:05.4	Henry Rono (Kenya)	1978
110 m hurdles	12.93	Renaldo Nehemiah (USA)	1981
400 m hurdles	47.02	Edwin Moses (USA)	1983
4 x 100 m relay	37.86	United States	1983
4 x 400 m relay	2:56.16	United States	1968
High jump	2.38 m (7' 9¾")	Zhu Jian Hua (China)	1983
Pole vault	5.83 m (19' 1½")	Thierry Vigneron (France)	1983
Long jump	8.90 m (29' 2½")	Bob Beamon (USA)	1968
Triple jump	17.89 m (58' 8½")	Joao de Oliveira (Brazil)	1975
Shot	22.22 m (72' 10¾")	Udo Beyer (GDR)	1983
Discus	71.86 m (235' 9")	Yuri Dumchev (USSR)	1983
Hammer	84.14 m (276' 0")	Sergei Litvinov (USSR)	1983
Javelin	99.72 m (327' 2")	Tom Petranoff (USA)	1983
Decathlon	8,779 pts	Jurgen Hingsen (FRG)	1983

Women	Record	Holder	When achieved
100 m	10.79	Evelyn Ashford (USA)	1983
200 m	21.71	Marita Koch (GDR)	1979
400 m	47.99	Jarmila Kratochvilova (TCH)	1983
800 m	1:53.28	Jarmila Kratochvilova (TCH)	1983
1,500 m	3:52.47	Tatyana Kazankina (USSR)	1980
3,000 m	8:26.78	Svetlana Ulmasova (USSR)	1982
Marathon	2:22.43	Joan Benoit (USA)	1983
100 m hurdles	12.36	Grazyna Rabsztyn (Poland)	1980
400 m hurdles	54.02	Anna Ambraziene (USSR)	1983
4 x 100 m relay	41.53	GDR	1983
4 x 400 m relay	3:19.04	GDR	1982
High jump	2.04 m (6' 8¼")	Tamara Bykova (USSR)	1983
Long jump	7.43 m (24' 4½")	Anisoara Cusmir (Romania)	1983
Shot	22.45 m (73' 8")	Ilona Slupianek (GDR)	1980
Discus	73.26 m (240' 4")	Galina Savinkova (USSR)	1983
Javelin	74.76 m (245' 3")	Tiina Lillak (Finland)	1983
Heptathlon	6,836 pts	Ramona Neubert (GDR)	1983

These records existed at the time of publication.